The Adventures of Kai and Nandini

A Beginner's Guide to Ayurveda

Written by Brittany Barrett & Lisa Lesser   Illustrated by Maggie Hurley

Shubha Publications, LLC
California, USA

Copyright © 2014 by Shubha Publications
All rights reserved. This book or any portion thereof
may not be reproduced or used in any manner whatsoever
without the express written permission of the publisher
except for the use of brief quotations in a book review.

Printed in the United States of America
Written by Brittany Barrett, www.DailyAyurveda.com
and Lisa Lesser, www.SeasonalWellness.com
Cover design, book design and illustrations by Maggie Hurley
www.MaggieHurley.com

Printed in the United States of America
First Printing: 2015

Shubha Publications
41 Via del Sol
Nicasio, CA 94946
ISBN-13 978-0-692-30541-6

We would like to dedicate this book to all of our teachers at Vedika Global, you have changed our lives in ways we could never have imagined. Shunya Pratichi Mathur Ji, Mahesh Sabade Ji, Abhijit Jinde Ji, Sanjai Mathur Ji, Tata Ji, Baba, and Bade Baba, we are overflowing with eternal gratitude. We would also like to thank our friends and family for your endless inspiration, support and encouragement.

Here is a boy named Kai, staring intently at the sky

Enjoying the clear warm summer night, gazing at the stars shining so very bright

A sparkling star falls at the speed of light

Bonks Kai on the head and everything is white

Floating around with ease and grace

Just a boy and his cow, lost in space

AAAAAAAAAAAAAAAAAUUUUUUUUUUUUUUUUUUUUU

UUUUUUUUUUUUUUUUUUUUUUUUUUUUUUUUUMMMMMM

Whoosh! A gust of wind is coming near
In a flash, the sky begins to reappear

Quick, cold, rough, active, and dry,
the breeze chills Nandini and sweeps away Kai

A warm gust of air creates a friction so outrageous

Starting a fire, also known as Tejas

Hot, bright, sharp, and spreading light

The fire inside them begins to ignite

The transformation runs through Nandini and Kai

Life giving nectar begins to fall from the sky

Cooling and sweet, delightful and fresh

All that is pure, all that is best

Settling into the ground, a sweet smell fills the air

The earth holds and supports them like a big, cozy chair

Rooting into the soil, solid , stable, and strong

Right back where Nandini and Kai belong

What a day, what a trip, what a journey it has been,
Feeling safe and sound, and relaxed from within...

Sipping spiced milk, all snuggled in bed,
rubbing his eyes, Kai finally rests his head.

Traditional Ayurvedic Spiced Milk

Serves: 2

2 cups Whole Organic Milk
1 cup Water
3 Cardamom Pods (crack pods open so the seeds are exposed)
1/4 teaspoon of Turmeric
1/4 teaspoon Ginger powder
1/4 teaspoon of Nutmeg (only add Nutmeg at night time - it acts as a mild sedative)
dash of Cinnamon
dash of fresh ground Black Pepper
4-5 strands of Saffron
Raw Sugar or Sucanat (optional)

1. Put all ingredients (except sugar) in a medium sized pot- on med/low heat, watch carefully and bring to a boil.

2. Simmer for 15 minutes. Boiling the milk with water will allow the herbs to saturate into the milk. Add sugar if desired.

Make it fresh every time. It's not ok to make a big batch and store it in fridge because the milk will become heavy and indigestible.

Each spice has unique beneficial qualities, and they all help balance out the heavy, mucus causing properties of the milk.

Basic Principles of Ayurveda

Ayurveda is a 5000 year old system of holistic health that originated in India. The word, "Ayurveda" is derived from the Sanskrit words "ayus" (life) and "ved" (wisdom). At the core of Ayurvedic philosophy is the idea that everything in the material world is made from five basic elements called the pancha mahabhutas. The five elements are akasha (ether/space), vayu (air), tejas (fire), aap (water), and prithvi (earth). Each person has a unique combination of these five elements in their body. We are not separate from our environment. In fact, everything that we come into contact with alters this sensitive elemental balance.

Each element has specific qualities, which are connected to our five senses.

Akasha- Ether/Space
Qualities: soft, light, subtle, expansive, porous
Sense: sound
Increases lightness, softness and porosity in the body
Food example: popcorn

Vayu- Air
Qualities: dry, light, cool, rough, subtle and mobile
Sense: touch
Increases dryness and lightness in the body.
Food Example: toast, broccoli, beans

Tejas- Fire
Qualities: Oily, Sharp, Hot, Light, Spreading
Sense: sight
Increases intelligence and metabolism, creates a healthy glow.
Food example: chili, ginger, mustard, garlic

Aap- Water
Qualities: cool, liquid, dull, soft, slimy, heavy
Sense: taste
Increases fluid content and lubrication in the body.
Food example: melons, cucumbers, juice, soup

Prithvi- Earth:
Qualities: heavy, rough, stable, solid, slow
Sense: smell
Gives structure and increases strength in the body.
Food example: meat, beets, bananas, wheat

About Brittany, Lisa, and Maggie

Brittany Barrett came to Ayurveda through her personal quest to seek natural healing from a chronic digestive disease. She discovered Vedika Global College of Ayurveda in 2009, and was fully cured soon after through following an Ayurvedic diet and lifestyle. Since graduating, Brittany founded Daily Ayurveda (www.dailyayurveda.com), a platform to educate people about the fundamental principles of Ayurveda and make it accessible and feasible for everybody to follow. Brittany is passionate about the healing properties of foods and spices, and enjoys cooking for her friends and family in her spare time. She also teaches cooking classes and provides personalized one on one health counseling.

Lisa Lesser is an Ayurvedic practitioner, wellness coach and postpartum doula. After the birth of her first child, it became clear to Lisa that the western medical establishment did not think about health the same way she did. She already had a budding interest in yoga (asana), food, herbs, nature and the power these things had over her health. Discovering Ayurveda gave her a construct to understand how these things fit together and a tool set to use them to help her family, friends and now her clients. After four years of course work at the esteemed Vedika Global and and two years of advanced clinical internship, Lisa is now helping Bay Area clients leverage the ancient teachings of Ayurveda to naturally lead healthier lives. Lisa lives in Marin county, CA with her husband, daughters, dog, goats and chickens.

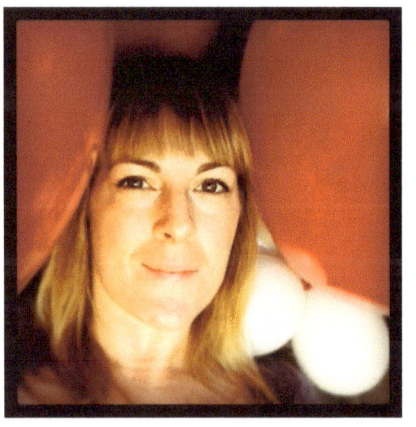

Armed with her grandmother's artistic proclivities, a stack of Brian Froud books, and some watercolors, Maggie Hurley taught herself to paint when she was a kid. She spent a year and a half at an art school in Southern California, which she adored, and has continued honing her skills ever since. She enjoys paint of all kinds and is especially happy to work on projects aimed at making the world a better place. She fimly believes in the healing powers of art and thinks we should all feel free to dabble without the fear of feeling like it's not going to turn out right. You can find more of her work at maggiehurley.com. When she's not painting, you can find her wandering the hills of the Bay Area with her overenthusiastic pup, Zoe, or curled up on a couch with her kitty, Miette.

www.ingramcontent.com/pod-product-compliance
Lightning Source LLC
Chambersburg PA
CBHW041544040426
42446CB00003B/224